D0037502

FORMULA ONE

You bring your car to a stop on the starting grid. Thousands of people are by the side of the track, and millions of others are watching on TV. Hundreds of people have worked on your car – designing it, testing it, moving it from track to track. Your team has spent millions to give you the best and fastest car; even the wheel in your hands cost thousands of dollars.

You think about the long story of Formula One, from the forty-eight hour race of 1895 to the ninety minute races of today. You remember the great names of the past, and the champions of today. You think about the other drivers – who will be the bravest today, or the cleverest, or the fastest? A few seconds pass.

And then the red lights go out, and there is only one thing to think about – winning the race . . .

CALGARY PUBLIC LIBRARY

JUN   2017

OXFORD BOOKWORMS LIBRARY

Factfiles

Formula One

Stage 3 (1000 headwords)

Factfiles Series Editor: Christine Lindop

ALEX RAYNHAM

Formula One

OXFORD UNIVERSITY PRESS

OXFORD
UNIVERSITY PRESS

Great Clarendon Street, Oxford OX2 6DP

Oxford University Press is a department of the University of Oxford.
It furthers the University's objective of excellence in research, scholarship,
and education by publishing worldwide in

Oxford New York

Auckland Cape Town Dar es Salaam Hong Kong Karachi
Kuala Lumpur Madrid Melbourne Mexico City Nairobi
New Delhi Shanghai Taipei Toronto

With offices in

Argentina Austria Brazil Chile Czech Republic France Greece
Guatemala Hungary Italy Japan Poland Portugal Singapore
South Korea Switzerland Thailand Turkey Ukraine Vietnam

OXFORD and OXFORD ENGLISH are registered trade marks of
Oxford University Press in the UK and in certain other countries

This simplified edition © Oxford University Press 2011

The moral rights of the author have been asserted

Database right Oxford University Press (maker)

First published 2011

10 9 8 7 6 5 4

No unauthorized photocopying

All rights reserved. No part of this publication may be reproduced,
stored in a retrieval system, or transmitted, in any form or by any means,
without the prior permission in writing of Oxford University Press,
or as expressly permitted by law, or under terms agreed with the appropriate
reprographics rights organization. Enquiries concerning reproduction
outside the scope of the above should be sent to the ELT Rights Department,
Oxford University Press, at the address above

You must not circulate this book in any other binding or cover
and you must impose this same condition on any acquirer

Any websites referred to in this publication are in the public domain and
their addresses are provided by Oxford University Press for information only.
Oxford University Press disclaims any responsibility for the content

ISBN: 978 0 19 423647 8

A complete recording of Oxford Bookworms Factfiles Stage 3 Formula One
is available on CD Pack ISBN: 0 19 423775 8

Printed in China

Word count (main text): 10645

For more information on the Oxford Bookworms Library,
visit www.oup.com/elt/bookworms

ACKNOWLEDGEMENTS

The publisher would like to thank Ben Michell, Senior Design Engineer, Dunlop Motorsport, for his expert advice.

The publisher would like to thank the following for their kind permission to reproduce photographs: Alamy Images
pp.18 (The Honourable Evelyn Ellis in Panhard Levassor 1895/Motoring Picture Library), 36 (Niki Lauda/Steve Yarnell),
40 (Michael Schumacher and Ferrari team/culture-images GmbH); Corbis pp.9 (Ferrari Formula One engineers check time
board/MAX ROSSI/Reuters), 27 (Formula One racing car crash/Schlegelmilch), 28 (Michael Schumacher at European Grand
Prix/Schlegelmilch), 52 (A McLaren Mercedes mechanic works on tyres/Jens Buettner/epa), 54 (Danica Patrick attends the
Izod Indycar Series celebration/Rob Kim/Retna Ltd.); Getty Images p.8 (Chevrolet 2011 Cruze ECO/Bill Pugliano); Jeremy
Griffiths pp.56, 60 (Karting); LAT Photographic pp.0 (2010 Belgian Grand Prix/Andrew Ferraro), 1 (Silverstone 1950, Giuseppe
Farina leads Luigi Fagioli), 3 (2010 Bahrain Grand Prix/Charles Coates), 5 (2010 Renault R30 Launch/Andrew Ferraro),
10 (Red Bull Racing RB6 Renault waits in garage/Charles Coates), 13 (Nico Hulkenberg, Williams FW32 Cosworth, on the
grid/2010 Malaysian Grand Prix/Glen Dunbar), 14 (Lewis Hamilton leads Toro Ross, 2010 Malaysian Grand Prix/Steven
Tee), 16 (2010 Monaco Grand Prix, Lucas di Grassi pit stop/Steven Tee), 17 (Mark Webber celebrates on the podium/World
Glenn Dunbar), 20 (Reims-Gueux, France, July 1939), 21 (Race winner Juan Manuel Fangio, Reims, France, 1951), 22 (Stirling
Moss, 1958), 24 (Lotus 72D-Ford Cosworth), 25 (Steering wheel of the Mercedes GP W01/Charles Coates), 29 (The safety car
leads, 2009 Shanghai International Circuit/Charles Coates), 32 (The Renault drivers train in Melbourne/Charles Coates),
35 (Peter Collins, Juan Manuel Fangio and Mike Hawthorn, 1957 German Grand Prix), 38 (Ayrton Senna celebrating victory,
1991 Brazilian Grand Prix), 42 (Jose Froilan Gonzalez and Luigi Villoresi head a group of cars, Monaco 1950), 43 (Aerial
view of the Istanbul Motor Park circuit/Lorenzo Bellanca), 44 (Yas Marina Circuit, Abu Dhabi/Steve Etherington), 46 (Lewis
Hamilton/Andrew Ferraro), 48 (Grid Girls, 2010 Spanish Grand Prix/Andrew Ferraro), 49 (Nelson Piquet Jr, Renault R28, 2008
Singapore GP/Glenn Dunbar), 49 (Broken bodywork from Renault car/Charles Coates), 50 (Marina Bay Circuit, Singapore/
Steven Tee), 60 (Crash barrier/Charles Coates); Oxford University Press pp.60 (Trophy cup/Photodisc), 60 (Formula One
driver/Randy Faris/Corbis), 60 (Fastening seat belt/Brand X Pictures), 60 (Desert landscape/Photodisc), 60 (Steering wheel/
Blend Images), 60 (Traffic through tunnel/Photodisc), 60 (Tyre/Ingram); Red Bull Photofiles p.55 (Red Bull F1 Showcar run in
Jamaica/GEPA pictures/Alfredo Martinez); Rex Features p.31 (Jenson Button karting/Chris Walker).

Diagram: p.7 by Peter Bull

Cover image: Getty Images (Formula One Grand Prix, Singapore/AFP)

CONTENTS

1 The greatest race

On 13 May 1950, twenty-one drivers started their engines at a race track in Silverstone, England. It was the first race in the new Formula One World Championship. Some of the cars on the track were made by car companies like Alfa Romeo and Maserati, but others were built by a few mechanics. They used engines from other cars, and they built their new cars for less than 2,000 dollars each.

Four red Alfa Romeo cars and their drivers – Fangio, Fagioli, Farina, and Parnell – were in front from the start. Fangio had engine problems and did not finish the race. Parnell's car hit a small animal on the race track, but he stayed in the race and finished third. Fagioli was second, and Giuseppe Farina won the race in two hours, thirteen minutes, and twenty-three seconds.

Farina in first place

Only twelve cars finished the race that day: the others had engine problems, fires, and accidents. The race was not on television, but about 120,000 people came to Silverstone to watch it. It was very dangerous for the drivers and for the crowd. People stood close to the track as the cars went past them at 160 kilometres per hour.

On 14 March 2010 at three o'clock, twenty-four cars waited on the track at the start of the Bahrain Grand Prix – the first race in the 2010 Formula One World Championship. Each car had cost millions of dollars to build. There were four world champion drivers on the track, and one of them was Michael Schumacher, the most famous racing driver in the world. One hour, thirty-nine minutes, and twenty seconds later, Fernando Alonso crossed the finish line to win the race. More than 50 million people were watching him on television.

When the drivers arrived in Bahrain a few days before the race, photographers and television reporters from all over the world were waiting for them. Today's Formula One drivers are as rich and famous as pop stars, but Formula One is a team sport. Teams of hundreds of people work for months to build the cars, and a 'track team', which can have as many as eighty people, helps the driver in the race.

Racing to the first corner
at Bahrain, 2010

There are hundreds of books, websites, and magazines about Formula One racing. More than 2 million people watch the races every year at the race tracks, and over 100 million people watch one race or more on television. So why is Formula One so popular?

Perhaps it is the speed of the cars, and their brave drivers. Today's Formula One cars race at over 300 kilometres per hour, and sometimes the drivers have less than a second to decide what to do. The smallest mistake can mean a terrible crash. That is what makes a Formula One Grand Prix the greatest race in the world.

2 What is Formula One?

There are lots of different car races, with different cars and different rules. Some races are on tracks, but others are on roads or even through fields. The International Automobile Federation (FIA) makes rules called formulas for some types of car race. What engines the cars can have, how big the cars are, how the drivers must race, and what technologies the teams can use – the answers to all of these questions are in the formula. There are different formulas for different types of car race, but the formula for some of the fastest and most powerful cars is Formula One.

The engines of the first Formula One cars were not as powerful as they are today, and the cars looked very different too. When car technology changes – sometimes as often as every year – the FIA changes the rules for Formula One. They do this to keep the races safe, fair, and exciting, but it means that the racing teams have to build new cars each time. If racing teams do not follow the new rules, their cars cannot enter the race. The rules that you read about in this book are the rules of 2010, but of course they may change every year.

The racing teams

Formula One cars belong to teams like McLaren, Ferrari, and Renault. The teams are also called constructors because they construct, or build, the cars. The racing teams have big factories, and their track teams, drivers, and cars travel around the world. Since Formula One began, there have been many racing teams. There are usually about twelve teams in the championship, and each team has two cars in the race.

Racing teams spend a lot of money, but they also get a lot of money from advertising and racing. Some big car companies like Ferrari and Mercedes have Formula One racing teams. Other teams like Williams only build cars for races. Some companies that do not usually make cars, like Red Bull, have racing teams to advertise their companies.

The Renault team, 2010

The circuits

Formula One tracks are called circuits. The circuits have straights, corners, and chicanes – two or more corners together, which makes cars go slower. Most circuits are about 5.5 kilometres long, and each time around the circuit is called a lap. Each Formula One circuit is different, but races are usually the nearest number of laps over 305 kilometres. For example, cars drive sixty-one laps to finish the 309.3 kilometre race in Singapore.

Just off the track is a place called the pits where teams have their garages. When drivers need to make a pit stop – to change their tyres, for example, or to fix a problem with the car – they move into the pit lane. This is a road next to the track, which takes drivers into the pits. They are usually back on the track about twenty seconds later.

The world championship

The first rules for Formula One racing were made in 1948, but the first world championship was in 1950. There were six races in Europe and one race in the USA that year. In 2010, there were nineteen races in eighteen different countries all over the world.

The first ten cars in each race get points for the driver and the racing team. The rules for points could change at any time, and have changed three times in the last twenty years. At the moment, the winning car gets twenty-five points, the second car gets eighteen points, and the tenth car gets one point. At the end of the championship, the driver who wins the most points wins the FIA Formula One World Championship. The racing teams get points from both of their cars, and the team with the most points wins the constructors' championship.

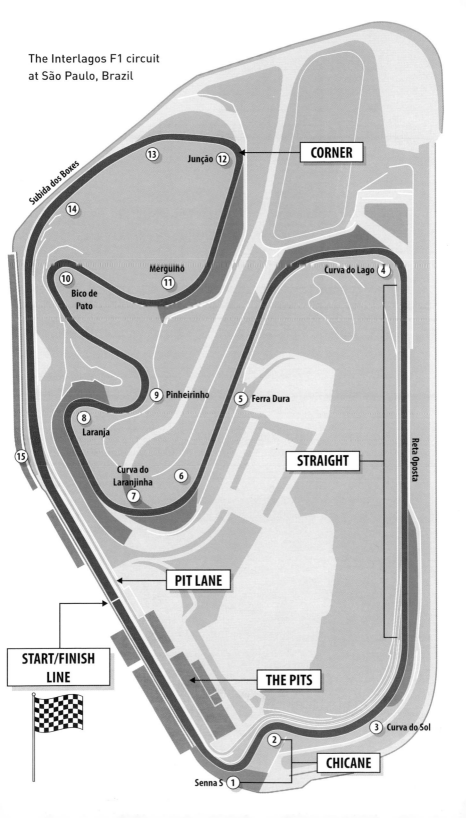

3 Inside a racing team

The last Formula One race of the championship is usually in November. A long time before that, the teams have begun to get ready for the next year. In the summer, the FIA makes the rules for the next year, and racing team designers start to design the new cars. It is very important to have the best car, so each Formula One team's designs are secret. The racing teams have very big factories: for example, five hundred people from all over the world work in one team factory in the UK. In the factories, different groups of people design and build the body, the engine, and other parts of the car.

How air moves over something like a car or a plane is called aerodynamics. A car has good aerodynamics if the air can move over and around it easily. Having good aerodynamics is very important in a race because it helps the car to move

Testing aerodynamics in a wind tunnel

Ferrari engineers watch tests on a Formula One car

fast, and to stay on the track. Most team factories use special rooms called wind tunnels to test their designs. In a wind tunnel, machines move air over models of the car. Parts of the car with bad aerodynamics are changed. To make the body of the car, engineers use a very light and strong material called carbon fibre. New carbon fibre parts are heated for hours to make them strong. To make all of the parts in time, the factories often work twenty-four hours a day.

Formula One cars have some of the best car engines in the world. Every year people make small changes to the engines, and this can take months. In the factory, computers test the engines at different temperatures and speeds. They use computer models of different race circuits to see how the engines will work in each one. The engineers make a lot of changes, and after each change they test the engines again.

When the car is ready, test drivers drive it on a track. They check how quickly the car can stop when the driver uses the brakes, how it goes around corners, and many other things. The drivers talk to the engineers and changes are made to the car. Different racing teams often test the cars at the same track, so it is a great chance to watch the other teams' cars.

The Red Bull team garage at the 2010 German Grand Prix

Each team takes a lot of people to the circuit for the race – perhaps as many as eighty people for a big team. Formula One circuits are all over the world, and teams have to move about 25,000 kilograms of parts and equipment to each circuit on time. Teams can only take two cars with them, but they can take a lot of extra parts. In one month, the teams may race in three countries in different parts of the world, like Korea, Brazil, and the United Arab Emirates. They have to find plane tickets and places to stay, and plan how to get everything that they need to each track – from engine parts, computers, and tyres to coffee cups, paper, and pens.

When the track teams arrive at the circuit, they have to build their team garages. Here they keep their equipment and get the cars ready for the race. The team garage has

places to keep parts, places for mechanics to work on the cars, places for engineers to sit at computers, and places for the drivers to rest. At some circuits the team garage is very small, so everything must be tidy and easy to find.

Different people in the track team do different things on race day. Mechanics fix the engines, engineers use computers to check the car, race engineers talk to the drivers in the race, and pit crews change the tyres.

Track teams practise for months to make sure that they can work quickly and safely: every second is very important in a race, and mistakes can be very dangerous. From March to November, the teams and drivers spend a lot of time together. They often see their team more than they see their families!

4   Race weekend

Formula One races are usually on Sundays, but things start to happen several days earlier. Pop bands play in the city, drivers talk to TV reporters, and rich people go to Formula One parties. At the track, the crowds can see the drivers practise, watch dancers, and look at Formula One cars from the past. There are often other car races too, like the Porsche Supercup.

Sessions on the track

A few days before the race, the drivers may walk around the circuit with their race engineers and discuss how to drive the race. They already know every part of the track because they have usually practised driving it on a computer. Then there are two types of session – time that the drivers spend driving on the track. Between Thursday and Saturday, there are three practice sessions. The drivers drive around the circuit to test the cars and think about how they are going to race. Where are the best places to overtake – to get past – other cars? What is the best way to get around each corner? At the same time, machines in the car called sensors send information about the car to the team engineers. How is the engine working? Are the aerodynamics correct for this circuit? How fast is the car on each corner? The engineers use this information to make small changes to the car before each race.

In the qualifying session on Saturday afternoon, the drivers race around the circuit and try to get the fastest time for one lap. Getting a fast time is very important because the cars start the race in different places. Lines on the track, called the starting grid, show where the drivers must wait at the beginning of the race. The fastest drivers start the race at the front of the grid, and the slowest drivers start at the back. The place at the front for the fastest driver is called pole position. After the qualifying session, the teams cannot make any more changes to their cars.

The race

About ten minutes before the start of the race, there are mechanics, photographers, engineers, drivers, and a lot of other people on the grid. The drivers are drinking water, walking around, or putting on their fireproof suits and helmets. About two minutes before the race, everybody

Niko Hülkenburg before the 2010 Malaysian Grand Prix

leaves the track, and the drivers are ready. When the green lights at the start line are turned on, they drive one lap to heat their engines and their tyres. Then they stop in their places on the grid. A few seconds before the race, the drivers are watching five red lights at the start line. The race starts when the red lights are turned off. Just 3.8 seconds later, the cars are moving at 160 kilometres per hour! They all want to overtake other cars before they get to the first corner.

Drivers go very fast on the straights, then use their brakes at the last moment to make the cars go slower at the corners. If a driver goes into a corner too fast, his car may start turning in circles or go off the track! Corners are good places to overtake other cars, but the driver in front may move across the track as he goes into a corner. This makes it more difficult for the car behind to overtake.

Lewis Hamilton in front at the 2010 Malaysian Grand Prix

Drivers often follow other cars very closely before they try to overtake. This is because more air hits the car in front and less air hits the car behind, so the second car can go faster. Sometimes the drivers make mistakes. They drive off the track, hit other cars, or crash into walls called crash barriers at the side of the track. When they crash, parts of the car can fly across the track and hit other cars.

The track team works very hard to help the driver in the race. Sensors in the cars tell the engineers things like how hot the tyres are, how well the brakes are working, how fast each lap is, and how much fuel the engine is burning. The race engineer gives the driver information about the car, warns him about problems, and tells him things like how far he is behind or in front of other drivers. He also talks to the driver about when to come into the pits.

Flags also give the driver information during the race. A yellow flag means that there is a problem on the track, and drivers cannot overtake. A red flag means the race has stopped, a white flag tells a driver about a slow car on the track, and a black flag tells him to leave the race.

Cars usually have between one and three pit stops in each race. The pit crew has about twenty people in it, and each person has a different job. It takes three mechanics to change each tyre, and they can do this in about four seconds. Other mechanics check the car, fix small problems, or tell the driver when to leave the pits. In the past, they put extra fuel into the car, but in 2010 the cars had to start with enough fuel for the race. The car can be back in the race just over twenty seconds after it drives into the pit lane. In that time, the other cars in the race can travel 1.5 kilometres!

Lucas di Grassi in the pits at Monaco, 2010

Choosing the right time for a pit stop is very important. If the car goes into the pits at the wrong time, it will go back onto the track behind a slower car. When it is going to rain, the team must decide when to have a pit stop and put on wet weather tyres. If they change the tyres too early, wet weather tyres will make the car slower. If it rains hard before they can change the tyres, it will become difficult for the driver to stay on the track. Engineers watch the weather every minute on their computers. They need to know what the temperature and the wind is like on the track, and when it is going to rain, how hard, and for how long.

It takes a fantastic driver and track team to win a Formula One race, but you also need a lot of luck. Other drivers can crash into you or you can hit something on the road. And in a race, the brakes and some parts behind the engine can get as hot as 750 °C! Because of this, the cars often have problems which mean that the drivers have to leave the race.

About one and a half hours after the start, a marshal waves a black and white flag as the winning driver crosses the finish line. Soon after the end of the race, he is given the winner's cup. But the drivers do not have a long time to rest. About ten days later, they will be in another country for another race!

Mark Webber with the cup after the 2010 British Grand Prix

5   How it all began

Only ten years after the first cars were made, people began to race in them. On 11 June 1895, twenty-five cars and their drivers left Porte Malliot, Paris, at the start of the world's first real car race. The race was from Paris to Bordeaux and back again, a distance of 1,190 kilometres. The cars raced through villages and towns, and along roads between farms.

French engineer Emile Levassor was the first to arrive at Bordeaux. A second driver was waiting in Bordeaux to drive the car back to Paris, but nobody could find him when Levassor arrived (in fact, he was asleep in a hotel). Levassor ate some sandwiches, had a short walk, and drove back to

A Panhard-Levassor car, 1895

Paris. News of his amazing drive reached Paris before him, and when he arrived on 13 June, thousands of people were there to meet him. He finished the race in 48 hours and 47 minutes, but he was nearly six hours in front of the next car. His speed over the race was just 24 kilometres per hour!

The first road races were started by French car companies. They wanted the races to show people that cars and not trains were a newer and faster way to travel. Companies worked hard to build better cars and win races. By 1901, cars had steering wheels, and air inside their tyres, and they reached speeds of 120 kilometres per hour. At these speeds on very bad roads, there were many accidents, but cars quickly became popular.

Gordon Bennett, an American newspaper owner, started a race called the Gordon Bennett Cup in France in 1900, and racing became international. Drivers from across Europe and even from the United States raced in the cup. The races helped car companies like Renault to grow and to sell cars.

In France in 1903, 13,000 cars were sold. In the same year, millions of people stood by the road in villages and towns to watch the cars race past in the Paris to Madrid international road race. There were no barriers in front of the crowds, and people ran into the road to watch the cars when they went past. Three drivers and two mechanics were killed in accidents on country roads, but the worst accident happened as the cars raced through the small French town of Châtellerault. A man tried to stop a child who ran onto the track. A racing car hit and killed them both, then drove into the crowd. Three people died and many more were hurt. The race was stopped that night in Bordeaux, and the cars went back to Paris by train. It was the end of city-to-city road racing.

After this there were circuits for car races. They used country roads and they did not have safety barriers, but these roads were closed to keep people, horses, and other cars off them. In 1906, the first French Grand Prix was held on a circuit of 104 kilometres of country roads around the town of Le Mans. In 1908, there was an American Grand Prix in Savannah, Georgia. There American crowds stood and watched as European racing teams took all of the first six places.

Car racing stopped for the First World War between 1914 and 1918. The first racing cars had been big and heavy, and they had huge 14 or 18 litre engines, but after the war, Italian companies like Fiat and Alfa Romeo designed much better cars. Their engines were smaller but more powerful, and the cars were much lighter too. Later, Adolf Hitler gave money to German car companies because he wanted to show the world that Germany was strong. By 1939, German companies like Mercedes Benz and Auto Union were building the best racing cars in the world. In tests, they reached speeds of 300 kilometres per hour. Then racing stopped again for the Second World War.

Auto Union cars in the 1939 French Grand Prix

Fangio winning the 1951 French Grand Prix

Grand Prix racing started again in 1946, and in 1948 the FIA made a new formula for racing cars: Formula One. At the time, Formula One cars could have big 4.5 litre engines or smaller 1.5 litre engines with a supercharger. A supercharger is a machine which pushes air into the engine to make it burn petrol better. In 1950, the Formula One World Championship began. Alfa Romeo cars won six of the seven races that year, and the real battle was between two Alfa Romeo drivers, Italian Giuseppe Farina and Argentinian Juan Manuel Fangio. Farina became the first world champion, but Fangio won the championship the next year.

Since the first Formula One races in the 1950s, car technology has changed a lot. The cars have become lighter, faster, and safer, and they have better aerodynamics. Each year, teams try to design the best cars. Each year brings new cars, new teams, new battles, and new champions.

6 Racing cars, then and now

In 1958, crowds watching practice sessions in Buenos Aires laughed at a 'funny' car on the track. Its engine was in the wrong place! The car was driven by British driver Stirling Moss. At the time, all Formula One cars had their engines at the front, but in Moss's car, the engine was behind the driver. The next day, Stirling Moss won the Argentinian Grand Prix.

Engines

Stirling Moss's 'funny' car was built by the Cooper racing team. Putting the heavy engine behind the driver in the middle of the car made it easier for Moss to turn at the

Stirling Moss wins in Argentina, 1958

corners. The front of the car was also lower, so it had better aerodynamics. Because of this it used less fuel, and this made it lighter and faster. Soon all Formula One teams put their engines behind the driver.

Racing teams are designing better engines all the time, but this means faster cars. Sometimes the FIA changes the rules about engines to make the cars slower and safer again. In the past, Formula One cars had much bigger engines. In 2010, Formula One cars used a 2.4 litre V8 engine. Each year clever engineers find new ways to make these smaller engines more powerful, so the cars go faster again. At the start of the race, today's cars can go from zero to 100 kilometres per hour in just 1.7 seconds!

Aerodynamics

When a car moves, the air pushes on it, so there is a force on the car. We call this force drag, and it stops things from going fast. The first Formula One cars had big, square shapes, so they made a big 'hole' in the air when they moved forwards. Today's cars are thin and have good aerodynamics. Air moves easily over the car, so there is less drag.

When racing cars go fast, the air moving around them can lift them off the track. How well a car holds onto the track is called grip. Good grip is very important at corners because the forces on the car try to move it in a straight line off the track. At high speeds old Formula One cars lost grip easily, and they often turned over and crashed. Then in 1968, a Lotus car appeared in the Monaco Grand Prix with two small wings at the front. Today, all Formula One cars have wings at the front and back. They are the opposite shape to aeroplane wings, and this means that air moves faster under the wing and slower over it. Because of this, a force pushes

**A 1972 Lotus car with
wings at the front**

the wing down. This is called downforce, and it keeps the car
on the track. Racing teams use computers and wind tunnels
to study how the air moves around and through their cars.
They want less drag to make the car move faster, and more
downforce to make the car stay on the track.

The cockpit

The first Formula One cars were built around a heavy metal
shape called a frame. They put the outside of the car onto
this frame. Then in 1962 Lotus built a car without a frame.
They used the outside of the car to hold it together. This
made the car much lighter. Without a big frame inside, the
cockpit was smaller, and the car had better aerodynamics.
The cockpit is the part of the car where the driver sits, and
in modern cars it is very small. The driver's seat is made to
the shape of each driver's body, and it is very close to the
ground. Drivers sit with their feet in front of them, so they
are nearly lying down. The cockpit is just big enough for the
driver's body, so the steering wheel is put into the car after
the driver gets in!

There was a big change to the cockpit in 1989, when Ferrari moved the gear levers of their car. Drivers use the gear levers to change gear and make the car go faster or slower. The new Ferrari had its gear levers on the steering wheel, so the driver could change gears much faster. He could also keep both hands on the steering wheel. Today all Formula One cars have seven gears to go forwards and one gear to go backwards. Drivers use the steering wheel to change gear, use the radio, and make small changes to things like the brakes. On the steering wheels the drivers can also see information and warnings about dangers on the track. Formula One steering wheels are much smaller than the steering wheel in a family car, but they cost over 30,000 dollars each!

A Formula One Mercedes steering wheel

7 Making the sport safer

On 19 June 1960, thousands of racing fans came to Spa-Francorchamps in Belgium to see the world's best drivers race on one of the fastest circuits in the world. It was a terrible weekend for British drivers. Before the end of the race weekend, two British drivers were killed in accidents, and two more were badly hurt.

At that time drivers did not wear safety belts, and there was nothing behind the cockpit to protect them when the car turned over. Drivers' helmets were very simple, and they were open at the front, so nothing protected the driver's face. When cars crashed, the fuel tanks broke and fires often started. Drivers did not wear fireproof clothes, and it was difficult to escape from the burning car.

In 1966, another British driver called Jackie Stewart was racing at Spa-Francorchamps when it started to rain heavily. His car went off the track, hit a wall, and turned over. He could not get out of the car. Two drivers managed to get him out of the car, but the ambulance did not arrive for twenty minutes. After this, Stewart and others fought to make Formula One safer. Things did get better, but after the terrible death of Ayrton Senna in 1994, people realized that much more had to change.

Today there are teams of doctors at the races and air ambulances to take drivers to hospital after a crash. Every 300 metres around the track a marshal is ready to help if

Luciano Burti crashes at the 2001 German Grand Prix

there is an accident or a fire. The cockpits and fuel tanks of cars are much safer, and Formula One teams have to do crash safety tests on their cars.

Materials like carbon fibre make modern Formula One cars much stronger. The drivers are often OK even after very fast crashes. There are many layers of carbon fibre around the cockpit, and these change shape when something hits them. This stops the force of a crash before it reaches the driver. The fuel tanks also change shape when something hits them, so they do not break. The shape of the cockpit protects the driver's head if the car turns over, and the sides of the cockpit are very strong. They could even stop a bullet!

Today's Formula One drivers wear five safety belts: two over the driver's shoulders, one around the middle of his body and two around the legs. A HANS device joins the back of the helmet to the safety belts over his shoulders and protects his neck in a crash. The cockpit is small, but the driver can get out very quickly. It only takes five seconds to take off the steering wheel, switch off the engine and fuel, open all five seat belts together, and get out of the car. If the driver is hurt, there are special places to hold on his clothing. Marshals can use these to pull the driver out of the car.

In the past, some drivers raced in T-shirts in the summer! Today's drivers wear fireproof clothes that are tested in temperatures of 800 °C. They protect the driver's body and head from a fire until the marshals can get to the crash. The shoes on his feet and the gloves on his hands protect him from fire, but they are also very thin, so he can feel the brakes and steering wheel.

Modern helmets are made of different layers of very strong and light materials. They protect the driver's head from fire and from things that may hit his helmet. There are also layers on the visor – the part at the front of the helmet that the driver looks through. When the visor gets dirty, the driver can pull off these layers and see clearly again. The helmets use amazing technology, but people still paint the advertising logos on them by hand!

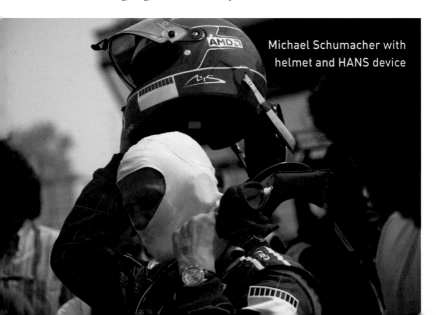

Michael Schumacher with helmet and HANS device

Drivers follow a safety car in wet weather

Rules make the sport safer too. Drivers must not drive dangerously or move too often across the track to stop cars which are overtaking. They must obey the flags, and they must not drive too fast in the pit lane. A safety car is used to start the race slowly when it is raining, or to stop the race when there is an accident on the track. When the safety car comes onto the track, the drivers must follow it and stop racing. When the safety car leaves the track, the race can begin again.

When drivers do not follow the rules, they are given penalties. In a ten-second time penalty, the driver must drive into the pit lane and stop for ten seconds. There are different types of penalties. If a driver does something really dangerous, the FIA can stop him from racing again.

Better cars and clothing, more marshals, and more rules have helped to make Formula One a safer sport, but it is still very dangerous. In July 2009, Brazilian Felipe Massa was driving in the qualifying session of the Hungarian Grand Prix when a piece of metal from another car hit the front of his helmet. He crashed at 270 kilometres per hour and nearly died.

8   Becoming a driver

In the cockpit of a Formula One car, the driver is nearly lying down. His feet are in front of him and his arms are next to his sides. He is travelling at 300 kilometres per hour and he is just centimetres above the track. He can feel everything that the tyres go over, and there is a very hot engine behind him. Inside the cockpit it can be 60 °C, and he is wearing a six-layer suit, a helmet, and gloves.

The race engineer is giving him information, but it is difficult to hear the radio because of the noise of the engine behind him. It is raining hard. Water from the car in front is hitting his visor, and it is difficult to see the track. He has to overtake the car in front of him, but it is harder to brake in the rain. He is driving down the straight as fast as he can. Braking at the last possible moment could get him past the car in front, or send him off the track. So what kind of person becomes a Formula One driver, and how do they learn to race?

Starting out

There is only one way to become a Formula One driver – you have to win races. Drivers race in other types of car for years before they get into a Formula One team. They have all been champion drivers in other races like Formula Three, GP2, or Formula Ford. Before that, most drivers have raced in karting.

World champion driver Jenson Button started to race in karts when he was just eight years old. In 1991, he won all

Jenson Button karting in 1994, when he was 14

thirty-four races in the British Cadet Kart Championship, and later he won the British Open Kart Championship three times. He drove in Formula Ford when he was just eighteen, and then in Formula Three. Racing teams sometimes give a Formula One test drive to successful young drivers. Jenson Button won a place in a Formula One team after three tests. In his third test, he raced a Formula 3000 driver for his place and won. The stories of most Formula One drivers are the same. They have all worked very hard, and they have all won a lot of races.

Driver fitness

In a Formula One race, a driver's heart beats about 190 times per minute. That is about the same as the heart of a runner in a 40-kilometre race. Formula One drivers have to be as fit as runners too. Racing teams have running and cycling machines that the drivers can use, and special machines to make their necks strong. Drivers do other sports too, such as running, cycling, and swimming. They want to be strong and fit, but they do not want really big shoulders, arms, or legs because they have to fit inside the cockpit.

Drivers need very strong necks when they are racing. When the car stops or goes into a corner, forces push their heads forwards or to one side. These are called g-forces. Normally a driver's head and helmet are nearly 8 kilograms. At a corner, the g-forces on the driver's neck may make his head feel like 32 kilograms. That is like lifting a heavy suitcase with your neck!

Formula One drivers running in Melbourne before the Australian Grand Prix, 2005

Most drivers prefer to eat healthy food, so team cooks make special food for them. In the days before a race, they eat different foods to give them lots of energy. Just before the race, the drivers drink a lot of water. In the hot cockpit, they lose a lot of water from their bodies. A driver can lose 3 kilograms in one race!

Getting ready for the race

People react when something happens. For example, when you fall, you react by putting your hands in front of you. In races, drivers react very quickly to what is happening around them. Drivers often use special machines and computer games to learn to react faster. They 'drive' the circuits on computers, and they also learn to see and drive the circuits in their heads. This is called visualization, and it helps them to do the right thing in the race.

Try to look at something very carefully for a few minutes, and see how difficult it is to concentrate on it for a long time. Drivers must concentrate on the track and the cars around them all the time in the race. Some drivers do Tai Chi or other exercises to help them to concentrate.

Just before the race, drivers often close their eyes, do exercises, or listen to music. This helps them to forget about everything before the race. When they are sitting on the grid, the TV cameras of the world and tens of millions of people are watching them. There is noise and colour all around them. They are just concentrating on five red lights at the start line.

9 Great drivers

When people think of Formula One's greatest drivers, they think of names like Juan Manuel Fangio, Niki Lauda, Ayrton Senna, and Michael Schumacher.

Juan Manuel Fangio

In just eight years of Grand Prix racing, Juan Manuel Fangio won twenty-four of his fifty-one races. He was world champion five times. Fans remember him most for the way he went around corners – very fast, with the car going across the track and smoke coming from the tyres!

Fangio was born in Balcarce, Argentina, in 1911. He started working as a mechanic when he was just eleven years old. In 1934, he built a Ford car from old parts, and he began to race. At the time, South American road races were thousands of kilometres long! Fangio became the Argentine national champion in 1940 and 1941, but he still worked as a mechanic.

Then in 1949, the Argentine Motor Club sent a racing team to Europe, and Fangio raced in Formula One cars for the first time. He quickly began to win Grand Prix races. The Formula One World Championship began in 1950, and in 1951 he became world champion.

In June 1952, Fangio missed a plane, so he drove through the night from Paris to a race at Monza, in Italy. He was very tired in the race, and he went off the track. Fangio was thrown out of the car and he broke his neck. The accident nearly killed him, but he got better. In 1953, he won the Carrera

Collins, Fangio, and Hawthorn at the 1957 German Grand Prix

Panamericana – a 3,000 kilometre road race across Mexico. Then Fangio won the Formula One World Championship every year from 1954 to 1957.

Fangio was forty-six years old when he won his last championship after a fantastic race in the 1957 German Grand Prix. His Maserati car was in front of Ferrari drivers Peter Collins and Mike Hawthorn when he went into the pits. After a slow pit stop, he came back onto the track thirty seconds behind them. There were eleven laps left in the race. In the next ten laps, he got closer and closer to the Ferraris. There was only one lap left. He went past Peter Collins as they came to a bridge which was just wide enough for two cars. Then he overtook Hawthorn on a very dangerous corner. His left tyres were outside the track on the grass! Many people call it the greatest Formula One race of all time. After the race, Fangio said, 'I have never driven that quickly before in my life and I don't think I will ever be able to do it again.'

Niki Lauda

After a terrible crash in 1976, doctors thought that Niki Lauda was dying – but just six weeks later, he was racing again.

Andreas Nikolaus Lauda was born in Vienna, Austria, in 1949. When he was seventeen, he went with some friends to watch the German Grand Prix at the Nürburgring. It was a day that changed his life. Niki decided that he wanted to be a racing driver. Racing is expensive, and Niki's family were rich, but at first they did not want their son to race. In 1968, he started racing in a Mini Cooper, but he did not tell his parents. He put the car in a garage at home and told them he was keeping it for a friend.

Niki raced in Formula Three, the Porsche Supercar races, and Formula Two. Then in 1971, he drove in Formula One for the first time. At first, he did not get any money for racing. In fact, he borrowed money from a bank, and paid teams to let him race in their cars! In 1974, he joined the

NIki Lauda in 1982

Ferrari racing team. He started to win races, and he became world champion in 1975.

On 1 August 1976, Niki was driving in the German Grand Prix at the Nürburgring when his car hit a barrier and started to burn. Other drivers pulled him from the car, but he had terrible burns on his body, head, and face. Doctors did not think he would live, but he got better. Niki still had a chance to be world champion that year, and he wanted to race again. He drove again in September at the Italian Grand Prix. It was difficult for him to open and close his eyes, and his head was bleeding, but he finished fourth!

The last race of that year was in October in Japan. Niki still had a chance to win the championship, but it was raining heavily that day. Niki could not see the track well because of the burns around his eyes, and he decided to leave the race. He lost the championship because of this.

In 1977, Niki Lauda became world champion for the second time. He stopped racing two years later, but he returned and won the championship again in 1984. Fans remember Niki Lauda because he drove bravely and well. After 1976 they always recognized him by the red hat that he wore. It hid the burns on his head.

Ayrton Senna

Ayrton Senna da Silva was one of Brazil's greatest sports stars. He became world champion three times and won his most famous race in his home country.

Ayrton Senna was born in São Paulo in 1960. He started racing in karts when he was thirteen and became the South American karting champion when he was just seventeen years old. Four years later, he moved to Formula Ford racing. Senna won five different racing championships in Formula

Ford and Formula 3 in only three years. Then in 1984 he joined a small Formula One racing team called Toleman. Toleman's cars were not as good as the big racing teams, but Senna drove very well, and people soon started to watch this exciting young driver. Later, Senna raced for bigger teams in better cars. He moved to Lotus and then to McLaren. He was racing for McLaren in 1988 when he won his first world championship.

Ayrton Senna was world champion again in 1990, but he had not won in Brazil. At the 1991 Brazilian Grand Prix in São Paulo, Senna started in pole position. It was a difficult

Ayrton Senna, winner of the 1991 Brazilian Grand Prix

race, but Senna fought hard and stayed in front. He was still in front when he had a problem – his gears started to break. In the next ten laps, he lost his third, fourth, and fifth gears. It became very difficult to drive the car, but he did not stop. Williams driver Riccardo Patrese was getting closer to him all the time. Senna drove all of the last lap with the car in sixth gear, but he reached the finishing line in front. He was too tired to get out of the car, so people lifted him out. Senna had won in his home town! That year, he became world champion for the third time.

For the next few years, Ayrton Senna was one of the best drivers in the sport, but other teams like Williams had better cars, and he did not win the championship again. On 1 May 1994, Ayrton Senna was in front of Michael Schumacher at the San Marino Grand Prix in Imola, Italy, when he went off the track. He hit a barrier at over 200 kilometres per hour and he was killed.

Michael Schumacher

Michael Schumacher has won more races than any driver in Formula One history, and he has been world champion seven times. For years, nobody could win against him. Schumacher was born in Hürth, Hermülheim, Germany, in 1969. He won his first karting championship when he was six years old! Later he won the German Formula Three drivers' championship and raced for Mercedes in the World Sportscar Championship. He started to race in Formula One in 1991.

After a few years, Schumacher was one of the best drivers in the sport. In 1994 he was racing for the championship against British driver Damon Hill. The last race of the year was in Australia, and Schumacher's Benetton car had

Schumacher and the Ferrari team in 2004

mechanical problems. When Damon Hill tried to overtake, Schumacher crashed into him. Both cars left the race, but Schumacher had more points, and he became the champion. Schumacher won the championship again with Benetton in 1995, and then he joined the Ferrari team. In 2000, he became the first Ferrari driver to win the championship for twenty-one years. He won for Ferrari again every year between 2001 and 2004.

Michael's brother Ralf joined the Jordan team in 1997. For the next nine years, Ralf and Michael raced for different Formula One teams. Sometimes both brothers were in front, fighting to win the race. In 2001, Ralf won the Canadian Grand Prix and Michael finished second. In 2003, Michael won in Canada and Ralf finished second.

Michael Schumacher stopped racing in 2006, but he tested Ferrari cars and worked with their drivers. Then in 2010, he returned to racing with the Mercedes team. He was forty-one years old. As he sat on the grid at the start of the first race, many people remembered the great Fangio, and how he had won the championship when he was forty-six.

10 The circuits

After the Second World War, the British Royal Automobile Club was looking for a place to start Grand Prix racing. They chose an old airfield near the village of Silverstone. The roads around the outside of the airfield were built for heavy planes, so they were great for high-speed racing. There was a farm in the centre of the airfield, and small animals called hares sometimes ran across the track. Now, more than sixty years after the first World Championship Grand Prix at Silverstone in 1950, they are still using the circuit, and the 'Silverstone hare' still appears sometimes.

In the first years of Formula One, the circuits were very dangerous. People stood next to the track as the cars raced past them at frightening speeds. There were not many safety barriers. Many of the circuits used country roads, so they were not very wide or flat, and sometimes there were trees and houses right next to the track. Today most circuits are much wider. There are strong safety barriers to protect the crowds, and 'run-off' places at the corners. These are places where a car can stop before it hits the barriers. The driver can then turn around and go back into the race.

Street circuits

Cars have raced through the streets of Monte Carlo, in Monaco, since 1929. Every year, clothes designers, film stars, footballers, and many more of the world's richest people come to Monte Carlo for the Formula One Grand Prix. People watch the race from expensive hotel rooms,

The Monaco Grand
Prix in 1950

from beautiful houses, and from the rows of million-dollar boats that come to Monaco.

In Monte Carlo, as the cars race down the hill at over 200 kilometres per hour, they brake at Mirabeau corner, go faster, then suddenly brake again to get around Grand Hotel corner, the slowest corner on any circuit in the world. They take it in first gear at about 48 kilometres per hour. After two more difficult corners, the cars go into the tunnel under the Hotel de Paris. When they come out into the bright light outside, they are travelling at about 280 kilometres per hour. Soon they have to brake hard again to go through the difficult left-right corners of Nouvelle Chicane. Monte Carlo is the most difficult and dangerous Formula One circuit in the world. In the city streets, there is no place for the cars to go off the track. If the drivers make a mistake, they will hit the barriers.

Today a lot of circuits are built near to big cities like Istanbul, Shanghai, and Kuala Lumpur, but they do not go through the centre of the city. However, city racing is becoming popular again. In 2010, there were street races in Melbourne, Monte Carlo, Valencia, and Singapore.

Designing modern circuits

On 21 August 2005, Kimi Raikkonen crossed the line to win the Turkish Grand Prix. It was the first grand prix race on the Istanbul Park track, and the drivers and crowds loved it. There were good corners for overtaking, some difficult chicanes, and long straights, where the cars reached 320 kilometres per hour. To make tracks like the Istanbul Park circuit, designers use ideas from famous tracks around the world. Parts of the Istanbul Park circuit are like Monza in Italy, Spa-Francorchamps in Belgium, and Interlagos in São Paulo, Brazil. Circuit designers want to make the track difficult but safe for drivers, and exciting for the crowds.

The Istanbul Park circuit in Turkey

Most circuits used to be in Europe, but now you can watch races all over the world, from Australia to the United Arab Emirates, and from Canada to Korea, and the newest circuits are some of the best. It took 14,000 people and 1.3 billion dollars to build the fantastic new Yas Marina circuit in Abu Dhabi. It uses ideas from street circuits like Monaco and Singapore. There is a hotel on a bridge over the circuit, shops and restaurants, a water park, and Ferrari World, where visitors can explore the world of racing, Formula One, and Ferrari. There are places around the circuit with trees and grass, but it does not usually rain in Abu Dhabi. They take the salt out of sea water and use it for the plants.

Getting the cars ready

Because each circuit is different, racing teams make changes to their cars before each race. Some circuits are flatter than others, so the teams make the cars closer to the ground if the track is flat, or higher if it is not. Before each race, the teams

The Yas Marina circuit in Abu Dhabi

fix the aerodynamics to get more downforce or less drag. On tracks with difficult corners like Monte Carlo, having more downforce is important because the cars can lose grip more easily at the corners. On tracks with longer straights, like Sepang in Malaysia, having less drag to go fast on the straights is more important.

The weather is very important too. In Abu Dhabi and Bahrain, the engines and tyres have problems in the hot weather, and sand can blow onto the track. The cars use different tyres and different fuel for different types of weather.

Racing teams use the practice sessions to see how the car is working on each track. After each session, they may make changes to the aerodynamics, the engine, the brakes, and the gears. It is very hard work to get the car ready for each race. On the night before the qualifying session, the circuit is quiet and empty, but lights are shining in the team garages. To get the cars ready for the track, some mechanics and engineers sometimes have to work into the night.

11   The racing business

In the 1950s, the best drivers in the sport were paid about ten thousand dollars a year. Today, racing teams pay some drivers between 10 and 25 million dollars a year, and in 2010 Michael Schumacher received 31 million dollars. Some teams spend several hundred million dollars to design, build, and race the cars. Where does the money come from?

The first racing teams were started by car companies to sell their cars. Later, racing teams put the logos of other companies on their cars to get things like free tyres and fuel. In the 1970s, Formula One races began to appear on television, and by the 1980s, all the races were on television. It was great for advertising, so cigarette companies paid money to the teams and put their logos on the cars.

Advertising logos on Lewis Hamilton's suit

Later, companies selling clothes, drinks, and lots of other things began to sponsor Formula One teams. Suddenly, Formula One was big business, and everyone wanted to put their company name on a car. Today, big companies like Vodafone and Petronas pay millions of dollars to put their names on Formula One cars, and on the driver's clothes and helmets. Some companies, like Virgin and Red Bull, have racing teams, which they use to advertise the company.

Since the 1980s, businessmen like Bernie Ecclestone have changed Formula One racing into a billion-dollar business. Today, TV companies around the world pay millions of dollars to show Formula One races. Other companies pay to put advertising around the track, or they sponsor different Grand Prix races. The racing teams get a lot of this money. The teams with the most points in the championship get the most money, but even the small teams get money for being in the race, and all the teams have sponsors.

Only a few sporting events are watched by more people than Formula One, and many of them, like the FIFA Football World Cup, only happen every four years. Formula One races happen about twenty times a year, and each race is watched by as many as seventy million people. Every year, companies find new ways to advertise to these people. Planes with logos on them fly over the circuit before the race, companies sponsor pop bands to play in the race city, and beautiful women called 'grid girls' walk around at the track with company logos on their clothes.

A Formula One race is great for the city too. A three-day race weekend ticket for a good place on the circuit can cost hundreds of dollars. Thousands of fans come to watch the race, and many of them stay in the city for a holiday. The hotels in the city are full and lots of businesses make money

Grid girls at the Spanish Grand Prix, 2010

from tourism. In 2005, the city of Melbourne in Australia made 54 million dollars from the Grand Prix, and 400 people found new jobs.

There is a lot of money in Formula One racing, but is all this money good for the sport? The big teams can make and spend more money, and many people think that this is unfair. A small racing team like Virgin spends about 60 million dollars to design, build, and race their cars, but the biggest teams can spend ten times more. The big teams use wind tunnels to test their car's aerodynamics, but Virgin uses computer programs because wind tunnels are too expensive. The big teams can make the best cars and they can pay the best drivers too. They win more races, and so they get more money from their sponsors. Some people want the FIA to make a rule about how much money the teams can spend on their cars. Some big teams do not want to do this.

Sometimes people may try to cheat. In 2007, information about the Ferrari team's car was found near the home of someone in the McLaren racing team. McLaren's engineers said that they did not see or use the information, but the team lost all of their points for that year, and they had to pay 100 million dollars as well!

In September 2008, the Renault driver Nelson Piquet Jr. crashed in the Singapore Grand Prix. Many people said that someone in the team told him to crash his car, but why? After the crash, the safety car came out onto the track, and the other cars went slower. The crash happened two laps after the other Renault driver, Fernando Alonso, had a pit stop. He was behind after the pit stop, but he caught the other cars when they were following the safety car. When the race started again, Alonso won. Later Piquet said that two managers had told him to crash. With so much money around in Formula One racing, some people may do anything to win.

Before and after
Piquet's crash

12   Into the future

With new rules, cars, circuits, and teams every year, Formula One changes faster than any other sport. How will it change in the future?

Night racing

On 28 September 2008, Fernando Alonso crossed the finish line to win the first night race in Formula One history. The Singapore Grand Prix started at eight o'clock in the evening. The cars raced between the tall buildings of the city centre and across two bridges. There were powerful lights around the circuit. The place of every light was planned to stop them shining into the drivers' eyes.

Night racing at the Singapore Grand Prix

Usually people can concentrate and react well in the morning, but they become tired and react more slowly in the afternoon and evening. This is because of their 'body clock', the natural way their body works at different times of the day. For the drivers at Singapore, who usually raced in the daytime, this was a problem. So before the Singapore race they slept all morning, had practice sessions late in the evening, and ate food at midnight. Because they did this, their body clocks changed. They were very awake in the evening, and this helped them to be ready for the night race.

Some drivers were worried about driving in the dark before the first Singapore Grand Prix, but it was a great success. It was good for business too. Racing at 8 p.m. in Singapore meant that it was the early afternoon in Europe and the morning in South America, so more people could watch the race. Now the Singapore Grand Prix is always at night. The Abu Dhabi Grand Prix starts as the sun goes down and finishes in the dark. In the future, we will see more night races in Formula One.

New countries

In 1950, there were six Formula One Grand Prix races in Europe and one in the United States. From the 1960s to the 1980s, there were more races in other places, like Brazil, Canada, and Japan, but most races were still in Europe. Most racing fans were European too.

By the end of the twentieth century, Formula One had become a true world sport. Today there are races all over the world, with fantastic new circuits in places like China, Korea, and the United Arab Emirates. In 2011, there will be a Formula One Grand Prix in New Delhi, India, for the first time.

Formula One will also return to America in 2012, and Cape Town may have the first race in Africa for many years. Countries like Russia, Mexico, Argentina, Egypt, Kazakhstan, Lebanon, and Qatar are all interested in having races too. We do not know where the circuits will be in twenty years' time, but there will be many new Formula One fans all over the world.

Formula One and the environment

Today's Formula One cars destroy lots of tyres and engine parts, and they use about 160 litres of fuel in every race. Making each car uses a lot of energy and materials, and racing teams fly people and equipment all around the world. Formula One racing is not good for the environment. But racing teams are always working to make Formula One cars work better, and this is good for the cars on our roads too. Today's family cars are safer and have better aerodynamics and engines because of technologies from Formula One racing. Because of this they use less fuel, and that is good for the environment.

A McLaren mechanic checks the tyres

When cars brake, the energy that the car has when it is moving is changed to heat. In 2009, some Formula One teams used a new technology called KERS. KERS takes energy from the brakes and saves it. The driver can use this energy later when he needs extra power. In the future, we will use KERS in many road cars. If we take energy from the brakes and use it again, we can save fuel.

Racing teams are starting to think of other changes too. Future Formula One engines will be smaller and they will burn less fuel. They may also use new fuels like bio-ethanol, which is made from plants. These things will be better for the environment.

Women in Formula One

There have only been a few women drivers in Formula One, and Lela Lombardi is the most famous. She raced in the world championship between 1974 and 1976, and finished sixth in the 1975 Spanish Grand Prix. No woman has ever won a Formula One championship race. Some people think that Formula One racing is more difficult for women because of the forces on the drivers' necks when they brake or go around corners. However, there are a lot of very successful women drivers in other car races.

Danica Patrick, Milka Duno, and Sarah Fisher race American Indy Cars. Indy Cars look like Formula One cars, and they often reach the same speeds too. In Japan in 2008, Danica Patrick became the first woman ever to win an IndyCar race. In 2009, she finished third in one of the most famous and most difficult races in the world: the Indianapolis 500. We may see Danica in a Formula One racing team one day, but why are there not more women drivers in Formula One?

Danica Patrick

Most drivers start racing in karts when they are children, and parents more often give boys the chance to do things like this. Because racing is expensive, drivers have to find sponsors, and it is often more difficult for women to find them. Championships like the IndyCar races have helped to change people's ideas about women drivers. Today more people are helping women drivers to start racing, and more companies are sponsoring them too. In the future more women will race in Formula One. Many people hope that one day a woman will be world champion.

13   Fast, dangerous – and exciting

Jamaica, in the Caribbean, is not famous for car racing. Although the island has a karting track, there is no Formula One circuit anywhere in the Caribbean. On a hot afternoon in May 2008, Sébastien Buemi drove a Red Bull Formula One car along Trafalgar Street in New Kingston, the Jamaican capital. There was only one car on the street, and Buemi did not drive very far, but he went as fast as he could on the short track. He turned the car around and around, and smoke came from the tyres.

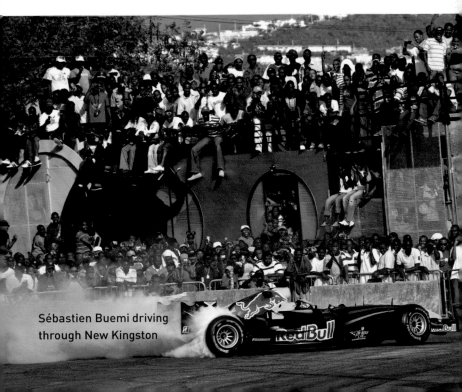

Sébastien Buemi driving
through New Kingston

Thousands of Jamaicans came and watched Buemi. They waited for hours in the hot sun for the best places. They wanted to hear the noise of the powerful engine, smell the burning tyres and see a real Formula One driver. They stood along the street, watched from roofs and windows, and climbed trees to get better photos. Children sat on their parents' shoulders and waved at the driver.

There are Formula One fans all over the world, even in countries like Jamaica, where there are no races. It is one of the world's most popular sports, because it is fast, dangerous, and exciting. And who knows? Somewhere under the bright sun in the thousands of faces along Trafalgar Street, perhaps there was the face of a future racing driver.

Future Formula One champions?

GLOSSARY

advertise to tell people about something you want to sell; (*n*) **advertising**

airfield a place where private planes take off and land

barrier something that stops people moving from one place to another

beat (of the heart) to make a regular movement

brake (*n & v*) to make a car go slower

champion the best player in a sport; (*n*) **championship**

concentrate to think carefully about just one thing

cup a large gold or silver cup given as a prize in a competition

design (*v & n*) to draw a plan that shows how to make something; (*n*) **designer**

energy power that you can use to do something, make something move etc.

environment the air, water, land, animals, and plants around us

equipment special things that you need for doing something

exercises something that you do to make your mind or body strong

fan a person who enjoys something very much

fitness being healthy and strong

force an effect that makes things move in a particular way

frame strong pieces of metal that give something its shape

fuel the liquid that is burnt to make a car go; **fuel tank** a metal box in a car that holds the fuel

gear a part of a car's engine that controls how fast it goes

Grand Prix a race in the Formula One competition

hare a small animal with long ears that can run very fast

helmet a kind of hard hat that protects the head

kart a small motor vehicle used for racing; **karting** the sport of racing karts

layer something flat that lies on another thing

logo a design that a company uses as its special sign

marshal a person who controls the crowds and deals with problems at sports events

material what you use for making or doing something

model a small copy of something used for planning or design

penalty a punishment for somebody who breaks a rule in sport

paint to put coloured liquid on something to change its colour

pit crew the people who work in the pits

point (*n*) a mark that you win in a competition

powerful having a lot of strength or power

practise (*v*) to do something again and again because you want to get better at it; (*n*) **practice**

protect to keep somebody or something safe

qualifying session the laps that decide where the drivers go on the starting grid for the race

race (*n & v*) a competition to see who can run, drive etc. the fastest

react to do something in answer to something that has happened

rule something that says what you must or must not do

run-off area a place where cars can leave the track safely

safety belt something that holds a driver safely in his seat to protect him in an accident

sand very small pieces of rock that you find on beaches

speed how fast something goes

sponsor a company that pays for a sporting event in return for advertising

steering wheel the wheel that the driver turns to make a car change direction

team a group of people who work together

technology using science to build and make new things

temperature how hot or cold something is

test (*v & n*) to use something to find out if it works well

track a special road made for cars to race on

tunnel a long hole under the ground for a road

tyre a thick rubber ring that goes on the outside of a car wheel

visualization seeing a picture of something in your mind

war fighting between armies of different countries

Formula One

ACTIVITIES

ACTIVITIES

Before Reading

1 Match the words to the pictures. You can use a dictionary.

barrier, cup, helmet, kart, safety belt, sand, steering wheel, tunnel, tyre

1 _____   2 _____   3 _____

4 _____   5 _____   6 _____

7 _____   8 _____   9 _____

2 Five of these people are famous in Formula One. Which ones are they? Which countries are they from?

Lance Armstrong, David Beckham, Jenson Button, Juan Manuel Fangio, Niki Lauda, Felipe Massa, Rafael Nadal, Cristiano Ronaldo, Michael Schumacher, Tiger Woods

ACTIVITIES

While Reading

Read Chapter 1. Complete the questions with the correct question words. Then answer the questions.

How many / What / Where / Who / Whose / Why

1 . . . was the first Formula One World Championship race?
2 . . . car had engine problems?
3 . . . happened to Parnell's car?
4 . . . was it dangerous for people in the crowd to watch the race?
5 . . . was the first race of the 2010 World Championships?
6 . . . world champion drivers were in the race?
7 . . . won the race?

Read Chapters 2 and 3. Then complete the sentences with the words.

aerodynamics, designs, formula, lap, material, pits, points, race engineer

1 A _____ is a set of rules for some types of car race.
2 Each time around the circuit is called a _____.
3 Racing teams have garages in the _____.
4 The first ten cars in each race get _____.
5 Racing teams keep their _____ secret.
6 _____ is how air moves over something like a car.
7 A lot of Formula One car parts are made of a _____ called carbon fibre.
8 A _____ talks to the driver during the race.

Read Chapter 4, then match these sentence halves.

1 At the practice sessions . . .

2 Drivers try to get the fastest time . . .

3 The fastest driver starts the race . . .

4 Drivers drive one lap to heat the car's engines and tyres . . .

5 The race starts when . . .

6 Drivers often follow other cars closely . . .

7 The cars have pit stops . . .

8 Flags give the drivers . . .

a) before they overtake.

b) in pole position.

c) five red lights are switched off.

d) information during the race.

e) in the qualifying session.

f) before the race starts.

g) drivers test the cars on the circuit.

h) to change tyres and make repairs during the race.

Read Chapters 5 and 6, then circle the correct words.

1 *Gordon Bennett* / *Emile Levassor* won the world's first real car race.

2 The winning car's speed was *24* / *48* kilometres per hour.

3 City-to-city racing ended after an accident in *France* / *Spain*.

4 After the First World War, racing car engines became *bigger* / *more powerful*.

5 A supercharger pushes *air* / *fuel* through a car engine.

6 The FIA created Formula One in *1948* / *1950*.

7 The first Formula One cars had their engines *behind* / *in front of* the driver.

8 Air moves faster *under* / *over* the wing of a Formula One car.

9 *Drag* / *Downforce* keeps Formula One cars on the track.

10 In 1962 Lotus built a car without a *frame / wing*.

11 Modern Formula One cars have seven *brakes / gears*.

Read Chapters 7 and 8 and answer the questions.

1 Who helped to make Formula One safer after a bad accident?

2 What happens to the fuel tank of a modern Formula One car in a crash?

3 How many safety belts do modern drivers wear?

4 How quickly can a driver get out of a Formula One car?

5 What must drivers do when the safety car comes out onto the track?

6 When did Jenson Button begin to race?

7 How is a Formula One driver like a 40-kilometre runner?

8 Why do drivers have to have strong necks?

9 How much water can a driver lose in one race?

10 What is visualization?

Read Chapter 9. Then fill the gaps with these names. Use each name twice.

Fangio, Lauda, Senna, Schumacher

1 _____ paid money to race in Formula One cars.

2 _____ raced against his brother.

3 _____ was killed in a race in Italy.

4 _____ drove in long road races.

5 _____ had terrible burns after a crash.

6 _____ won a very difficult race in his home city.

7 _____ won a championship when he was a young child.

8 _____ built a racing car.

Read Chapters 10 and 11. Use the numbers to complete the sentences.

seventy, fourteen thousand, thirty-one, three hundred and twenty, four hundred, forty-eight

1 In Monte Carlo, the cars have to drive around Grand Hotel corner at just _____ kilometres per hour.
2 At the Istanbul Park Circuit, cars can travel at speeds of _____ kilometres per hour.
3 It took _____ workers to build the Yas Marina Circuit, in Abu Dhabi.
4 Michael Schumacher got _____ million dollars for driving in 2010.
5 As many as _____ million people watch each Formula One race on TV.
6 In 2005, about _____ people found new jobs in Melbourne because of the Australian Grand Prix.

Read Chapters 12 and 13. Rewrite these untrue sentences with the correct information.

1 People in Europe can watch the Singapore Grand Prix in the morning in their own countries.
2 In the 1950s, most Formula One races were in America.
3 KERS technology helps to keep the driver safe.
4 Future Formula One engines will burn more fuel.
5 Women drivers have won a lot of Formula One championship races.
6 You cannot go to watch karting or Formula One races anywhere in the Caribbean.
7 People waited for hours to race against Sébastien Buemi in Jamaica.

ACTIVITIES

After Reading

1 Use the clues below to complete the puzzle with words from
Formula One. Then find the hidden nine-letter word.

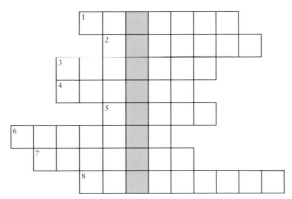

1 The driver sits in this.
2 A place on the track where there are two corners together.
3 A driver gets this if he does something wrong in the race.
4 The driver wears this on his head.
5 How fast something is.
6 Another word for 'race track'.
7 Machines inside the car which send information.
8 Another word for 'build'.

The hidden word is _____ .
The person who is this in Formula One today is _____ .
I think the greatest one of these in Formula One is
_____ because _____ .

2 One word in each group (1–5) belongs to a different group. Find these words and move each one to the correct group.

1 _____: designer, drag, engineer, mechanic
2 _____: brakes, company, steering wheel, tyres
3 _____: advertising, logo, pit crew, sponsor
4 _____: engine, pit lane, safety barrier, start grid
5 _____: corner, downforce, grip, wind tunnel

Then choose one of these headings for each group.

aerodynamics, big business, car parts, circuits, racing teams

3 **Complete the sports commentaries from two Grand Prix races with these words.**

barrier, behind, Champion, corners, drivers, flags, grip, helmet, lap, marshals, mistake, overtake, pits, safety, track, tyres

Brazil 2008

'Glock didn't go into the _____ to change his _____. That was a _____, because now he's losing _____ in the rain. Hamilton's right _____ him as they race towards the last two _____ of the circuit. Yes! He's gone past! Lewis Hamilton has become World _____ on the last _____ in the last race of the year – I've never seen anything like it!'

Monaco 2010

'Barichello has hit the crash _____. He's out of the race. He's taken off his _____ and he looks OK, but there are parts of his car on the _____. The _____ are trying to pick them up and the _____ car has come out onto the circuit. I can see yellow _____ everywhere. All the _____ are slowing down now. They can't _____.'

4 Do you agree or disagree with these statements? Why?

1 Formula One drivers had to be braver in the past.

2 Car racing is bad for the environment.

3 The FIA should stop the big teams from spending so much money on their cars.

4 Michael Schumacher is the greatest driver in the history of the sport.

5 Formula One technology will help us all in the future.

6 Women racing drivers will never be as successful as men in Formula One.

7 Formula One isn't as exciting as football.

8 Having the best car is more important than being the best driver.

9 There are too many rules in Formula One.

5 Write a short biography of a driver or prepare a short presentation on a Formula One driver for your class. Use the internet and think about these questions.

- What cars did he/she race in before driving in Formula One?
- What are his/her greatest successes?
- What interesting information do you know about the driver's personal life?

These websites can help you:
http://www.formula1.com, http://news.bbc.co.uk/sport,
http://www.f1technical.net

Formula One racing teams also have good websites, for example: http://www.redbullracing.com,
http://mclaren.com, http://www.thescuderia.net,
http://www.mercedes-gp.com

ABOUT THE AUTHOR

Alex Raynham first began to follow Formula One racing after getting to know a member of the Honda (now Mercedes GP) racing team. Over time, he became a big fan of the sport, and now he tries hard to watch every race. He shares his interest with his sister Sally. They both admire British driver Lewis Hamilton, who became the sport's youngest ever world champion in 2008 when he was just twenty-three years old.

Alex has taught English in Italy, the UK and Turkey. He has also travelled around the world, seeing some of the world's most beautiful places. In the last ten years, Alex has worked on many books for Oxford University Press, and has written graded readers for Oxford Read and Discover as well as Factfiles. He now lives with his wife Funda in Adana, Turkey, next to a lake and near to the beautiful southern Turkish coast.

In his spare time, Alex enjoys oil painting, wildlife watching, walking, swimming, and watching sports like Formula One and football.

OXFORD BOOKWORMS LIBRARY

Classics • Crime & Mystery • Factfiles • Fantasy & Horror
Human Interest • Playscripts • Thriller & Adventure
True Stories • World Stories

The OXFORD BOOKWORMS LIBRARY provides enjoyable reading in English, with a wide range of classic and modern fiction, non-fiction, and plays. It includes original and adapted texts in seven carefully graded language stages, which take learners from beginner to advanced level. An overview is given on the next pages.

All Stage 1 titles are available as audio recordings, as well as over eighty other titles from Starter to Stage 6. All Starters and many titles at Stages 1 to 4 are specially recommended for younger learners. Every Bookworm is illustrated, and Starters and Factfiles have full-colour illustrations.

The OXFORD BOOKWORMS LIBRARY also offers extensive support. Each book contains an introduction to the story, notes about the author, a glossary, and activities. Additional resources include tests and worksheets, and answers for these and for the activities in the books. There is advice on running a class library, using audio recordings, and the many ways of using Oxford Bookworms in reading programmes. Resource materials are available on the website <www.oup.com/elt/bookworms>.

The *Oxford Bookworms Collection* is a series for advanced learners. It consists of volumes of short stories by well-known authors, both classic and modern. Texts are not abridged or adapted in any way, but carefully selected to be accessible to the advanced student.

You can find details and a full list of titles in the *Oxford Bookworms Library Catalogue* and *Oxford English Language Teaching Catalogues*, and on the website <www.oup.com/elt/bookworms>.

THE OXFORD BOOKWORMS LIBRARY
GRADING AND SAMPLE EXTRACTS

STARTER • 250 HEADWORDS

present simple – present continuous – imperative –
can/cannot, must – *going to* (future) – simple gerunds …

Her phone is ringing – but where is it?

Sally gets out of bed and looks in her bag. No phone. She looks under the bed. No phone. Then she looks behind the door. There is her phone. Sally picks up her phone and answers it. *Sally's Phone*

STAGE 1 • 400 HEADWORDS

… past simple – coordination with *and, but, or* –
subordination with *before, after, when, because, so* …

I knew him in Persia. He was a famous builder and I worked with him there. For a time I was his friend, but not for long. When he came to Paris, I came after him – I wanted to watch him. He was a very clever, very dangerous man. *The Phantom of the Opera*

STAGE 2 • 700 HEADWORDS

… present perfect – *will* (future) – *(don't) have to, must not, could* –
comparison of adjectives – simple *if* clauses – past continuous –
tag questions – *ask/tell* + infinitive …

While I was writing these words in my diary, I decided what to do. I must try to escape. I shall try to get down the wall outside. The window is high above the ground, but I have to try. I shall take some of the gold with me – if I escape, perhaps it will be helpful later. *Dracula*